2018

Happy Birthday, Ellen!

Love,
Diane

FLYING ABOVE

CHESAPEAKE BAY

PHOTOGRAPHY BY

JAKE McGUIRE

NARRATIVE BY

ANNA KATALKINA

First published in the United States of America by:

Twin Lights Publishers, Inc.
8 Hale Street
Rockport, Massachusetts 01966
Telephone: (978) 546-7398
http://www.twinlightspub.com

ISBN: 978-1-885435-93-4
ISBN: 1-885435-93-2

10 9 8 7 6 5 4 3 2 1

(opposite)
Western Shore, Kent Island, Maryland

(frontispiece)
Chesapeake Bay Bridge at Sunset

(jacket front)
Queen Anne Marina, Stevensville, Kent Island, Maryland

(jacket back)
Senator William V. Roth, Jr. Bridge (cable-stayed) and St. Georges Bridge (arch span), Chesapeake and Delaware Canal

Book design by:
SYP Design & Production, Inc.
www.sypdesign.com

Printed in China

INTRODUCTION

For thousands of years, beginning long before the first European explorers arrived, the scenic vistas and rich natural resources of the Chesapeake Bay have lured settlers to its shores. The vast estuary is the largest in the United States. Much of our nation's history began here, and it comes to life in the many carefully preserved historic districts along its border. Fort Monroe, in Hampton, Virginia played a strategic role in both the Revolutionary War and the Civil War. In World War II, it became home to the U.S. Army Training and Doctrine Command. St. Mary's City, Maryland was one of the first Catholic settlements in the New World. Annapolis, Maryland takes pride in the oldest state house still in legislative use, and claims the greatest concentration of original 18th century buildings in America. St. Michaels hosts the Chesapeake Bay Maritime Museum in honor of its early shellfish harvesting and boat-building traditions.

Geologically, the Chesapeake Bay is a *ria*, or drowned valley, of the Susquehanna River, which stretches some 200 miles from Havre de Grace, Maryland to Virginia Beach, Virginia. Its watershed covers 64,000 square miles, also impacting Delaware, West Virginia, New York and Washington, D.C. Two dramatic bridges span the Chesapeake Bay, transporting more than 25 million vehicles a year bound for popular Atlantic Ocean resorts. The Chesapeake Bay Bridge connects the Washington-Baltimore-Annapolis area to Kent Island, Maryland, and the Chesapeake Bay Bridge-Tunnel links Hampton Roads and Cape Charles, Virginia.

Vacationers flock to the Chesapeake Bay for its endless recreational possibilities, from fishing and hunting to camping, boating and swimming, as well as sightseeing and fine dining in the historic towns of St. Michaels, Irvington, Easton and others. Whether they come for a round-the-world sailing race or to spend the day in a secluded cove, to stroll a historic cobblestone street, watch fishermen at work, or feast on famous Chesapeake Bay blue crabs, there is enjoyment for millions of visitors from the United States and around the world.

The Chesapeake Bay is a very complex and fragile ecosystem, home to thousands of species of flora and fauna. For nearly 30 years, the Chesapeake Bay Foundation and other concerned organizations have set an example for environmental action as they work tirelessly to restore health to endangered marine zones and preserve the beloved Chesapeake Bay for the future generations.

This collection of photographs is a tribute to the beauty of the Chesapeake Bay, its tributaries and islands, its history and culture. We invite you to join award-winning photographer Jake McGuire in a breathtaking aerial tour of our great natural treasure.

Blackwater National Wildlife Refuge
Tidal Marshes

At the meeting of land and water, two ecosystems collaborate to create one of nature's loveliest works of art. Blackwater National Wildlife Refuge in Cambridge, Maryland is a spectacular vantage point to observe thousands of migratory waterfowl traveling along the Atlantic Flyway. The 27,000-acre area is composed mainly of tidal salt marshes and offers hiking and paddling trails, cycling roads, and hunting and fishing opportunities.

OPPOSITE: VIRGINIA BEACH AND RUDEE INLET, VIRGINIA • ABOVE: CAPE HENRY, VIRGINIA BEACH, VIRGINIA

Virginia Beach

Miles of surf and sand, beachfront hotels, and restaurants make Virginia Beach one of the most popular seaside destinations on the Atlantic coastline. Rudee Inlet provides the only ocean access for boats along the Virginia Beach coastline. Its sheltered harbor is home to yachts, fishing boats, and other recreational vessels, as well as whale watching charters.

Cape Henry Light

The Virginia coast is the site of hundreds of shipwrecks. The first Cape Henry Lighthouse was built of brick in 1792 at Fort Story as a beacon to the growing number of merchant ships entering Chesapeake Bay. The second lighthouse, built in 1881 at 163 feet, is the tallest cast-iron plate lighthouse in the United States. The two lighthouses stand just 350 feet apart.

TOP AND BOTTOM: ELIZABETH RIVER, NORFOLK, AND PORTSMOUTH, VIRGINIA • OPPOSITE: NAVAL STATION NORFOLK, NORFOLK, VIRGINIA

Maritime Hub

The largest base for the United States Navy is sheltered in the deep waters of the Elizabeth River. Since the 17th century, the Port of Virginia has been a hub of military and commercial maritime operations. U.S. Navy and commercial contractor docks, industrial plants and coal loading operations line the historic waters. Constant silting has required frequent dredging to keep the river open. The Elizabeth River is currently twice its original depth, but it has lost a third of its width.

Homecoming

Tugboats create huge fountains of water to greet warships returning to Naval Station Norfolk. Sailors and officers in full white dress uniform line the decks in salute as each ship returns after as long as two years away from home. This memorable sight is best observed from the water, at the entrance to the Elizabeth River.

M
MARCI MORAN

VIRGINIA PORT AUTHORITY, PINNER POINT, NORFOLK, VIRGINIA

Pinner Point

The Virginia Port Authority operates the region's major marine cargo terminals that include Norfolk International Terminals (NIT), Newport News Marine Terminal, Portsmouth Marine Terminal and the Virginia Inland Port, in Front Royal. The 219 foot tall Suez-class container cranes at NIT are the tallest in the world.

WATERFRONT, PORTSMOUTH, VIRGINIA

Portsmouth Waterfront

Portsmouth has been a crucial East Coast port since the historic city was founded in 1752. Modern revitalization along the shores of the Elizabeth River has brought in high-rise hotels and condominiums, which provide majestic views of the river and downtown Norfolk.

TOP: LAMBERTS POINT COAL TERMINAL, NORFOLK, VIRGINIA • BOTTOM: NAVAL MEDICAL CENTER, PORTSMOUTH, VIRGINIA

Half A Million Tons

Lamberts Point Coal Terminal is the largest coal trans-loading terminal in the Northern Hemisphere. The adjacent Lambert's Point Docks, Virginia's largest break-bulk marine terminal, processes thousands of rail cars delivering rubber, cocoa, and other shipments from around the world totaling over half a million tons of cargo each year.

Oldest Navy Hospital

Naval Medical Center Portsmouth, the nation's oldest United States Navy hospital, is located on the banks of the Elizabeth River, where Fort Nelson stood in the 18th century. Today, this state-of-the-art facility, equipped with cutting edge technology and staffed with superior medical personnel, continues to provide care to the military and their families.

FORT MONROE, HAMPTON, VIRGINIA

Fort Monroe

Named in honor of President James Monroe, this massive, multi-sided structure is the largest stone fort in the country. Built in 1834 and surrounded by a medieval-style moat, Fort Monroe was designed to guard the mouth of Hampton Roads from foreign fleets. It remains an active Army post. The Casemate Museum is open for tours.

OLD PORT COMFORT, HAMPTON, VIRGINIA

Old Point Comfort Lighthouse

The Old Point Comfort Light at Fort Monroe is rich in American history. During the War of 1812, the British captured the tower and used it as an observation point to monitor Norfolk. At the end of the Civil War, Confederate President Jefferson Davis was imprisoned in a building behind the light. Old Point Comfort Light, automated in 1973, is still active.

HAMPTON ROADS, HAMPTON, VIRGINIA

Hampton Harbor Fishing Boats

A variety of commercial fishing vessels and pleasure craft sail out of Hampton Harbor, at the mouth of the Chesapeake Bay. Established in 1610, Hampton is one of the best-kept secrets on the East Coast.

ABOVE AND OPPOSITE: CHESAPEAKE BAY TO ELIZABETH RIVER, NORFOLK, VIRGINIA

Sail Virginia

More than 50 tall ships from around the world marked the 400th anniversary of the founding of Jamestown with a six-day maritime spectacle, Sail Virginia. The event was also held in conjunction with Norfolk's annual, three-day Harborfest. The parade of ships began in the lower Chesapeake Bay off Ocean View and ended with a dramatic sail up the Elizabeth River. Hundreds of local boats and thousands of land-side spectators followed the progress of the fully rigged sailing ships, sleek schooners and small ketches.

Jamestown
VIRGINIA

VIRGINIA

OPPOSITE AND ABOVE: ELIZABETH RIVER, PORTSMOUTH, NORFOLK, VIRGINIA

Tall Ships

The tall ships docked at Norfolk's Town Point Park, thrilled tourists and locals with a forest of masts; a rare sight not unlike the waterfront of 200 years ago. Tugboats led the official parade of tall ships up the Elizabeth River. Sail Virginia was conceived to promote the 400th anniversary of the Jamestown Colony, the spirit of Norfolk and Virginia's rich history.

TOWN POINT PARK, NORFOLK, VIRGINIA

Week-Long Festival

In addition to the tall ships from around the world, Native Americans convened from throughout Virginia to celebrate their critical role in Virginia's history during Sail Virginia. The festival drew in hundreds of artists, musicians, and craftsmen. Historical re-enactments, military parades, and fireworks charged the festive atmosphere with excitement.

WATERSIDE DOCK, NORFOLK, VIRGINIA

State-of-the-Art Cruise Port

The deep waters of the Elizabeth River have been used for navigation since the region's Colonial Period. Named for a 17th-century fort, the Half Moone Cruise and Celebration Center is an 80,000 square-foot cruise facility. The terminal accommodates liners sailing to The Bahamas, Bermuda, the Caribbean, New England and Canada.

OPPOSITE, TOP: GEORGE P. COLEMAN MEMORIAL BRIDGE, YORKTOWN • OPPOSITE, BOTTOM: GLOUCESTER POINT, VIRGINIA • ABOVE: SARAH'S CREEK, YORK RIVER, GLOUCESTER POINT, VIRGINIA

Double-Swing-Span Bridge

The 3,750 foot-long Coleman Bridge is a double-swing-span bridge that connects York and Gloucester counties over the York River. Soaring about 90 feet above the water, it swings open to handle large commercial and military traffic on the river. Built in 1952, the Coleman Bridge was widened in 1995 to accommodate growing commuter needs.

Virginia Institute of Marine Science

VIMS, a professional graduate school for the College of William and Mary, is among the largest marine research and education centers in the United States. It was chartered in 1940 to provide research, education, and expertise in contemporary marine science. Its 35-acre main campus is located on Gloucester Point, Virginia.

Sarah's Creek

A tributary of the lower York River, Sarah's Creek flows to the east of Gloucester Point. It played key roles during both the Revolutionary and Civil Wars, as the site of fortifications against adversarial ships on the York River. Commercial oyster production, once an important part of the local economy, has been replaced by residential growth and development.

ABOVE: ENTRANCE TO PERRIN RIVER, HAYES, VIRGINIA • OPPOSITE: NEW POINT COMFORT LIGHT, MOBJACK BAY, VIRGINIA

Protected Harbor

Great fishing spots, sailing, and immediate access to the Chesapeake Bay make Perrin River, near the mouth of the York River, popular with recreational boaters. Crown Pointe Marina, with its protected harbor just past Jenkins Neck, makes a good starting point for many boaters.

New Point Comfort Light

Built in 1805 by Elzy Burroughs, builder of the Old Point Comfort Light, this 55-foot-high sandstone tower stood on land at the entrance of Mobjack Bay until the Hurricane of 1933. The third oldest lighthouse on the Chesapeake Bay now stands alone, a watchful sentry on its own tiny island in the bay.

ABOVE: DYER CREEK, NEW POINT COMFORT, VIRGINIA • OPPOSITE, TOP: NEW POINT, VIRGINIA • OPPOSITE, BOTTOM: CRICKET HILL AND GWYNN'S ISLAND, VIRGINIA

Idyllic Peninsula

The natural beauty of this peninsula inspired plans, in the 1900s, for an idyllic seaside resort, with a grand hotel near the Old Point Comfort Light at its tip. Marshes were to be filled and beaches expanded. Prohibitive costs doomed the project, which was fortunate, as the Hurricane of 1933 would have blown much of it away.

Campsites

Soft white sands, calm waters, pristine nature, and gorgeous views of the Chesapeake Bay attract down-to-earth vacationers. A popular campground destination at New Point offers swimming, fishing, boating, crabbing, and clamming at their tent and RV camping sites.

Battle Site

In July of 1776, a battery stood on Cricket Hill, facing Gwynn's Island, where the Colonial Governor, Lord Dunmore, had set up a British camp to fight off the Virginia forces. Virginia won the Battle of Cricket Hill, forcing the British to evacuate the island.

STINGRAY POINT, DELTAVILLE, VIRGINIA

Healing History

Back in the 1600s, Captain John Smith was seriously injured by a stingray. He was cured by the Indians, and the site of the healing was named Stingray Point. Nestled at the eastern-most tip of the Middle Peninsula on Virginia's Coastal Plain, Stingray Point marks the entrance of two rivers: the Rappahannock on the north and the Piankatank on the south.

TOP AND BOTTOM: HUNTING AND STURGEON CREEKS, DELTAVILLE, VIRGINIA

Boat Building History

Once the boat-building capital of the Chesapeake Bay, Deltaville has evolved into a favorite recreational destination. Its rivers, creeks, and marshes provide a rich habitat for wildlife. Deltaville's population more than quadruples in summer as vacationers flock in for fishing tournaments, sailboat races, seafood festivals, and fireworks.

MEACHIM CREEK, TOPPING, VIRGINIA

Meachim Creek

This quiet community on Meachim Creek, located between Urbanna and Deltaville and across the river from White Stone, offers good fishing and sailing on the lower Rappahannock River. Hummel Field Airport is visible just behind the creek.

TOP: URBANNA CREEK, URBANNA, VIRGINIA • BOTTOM: LOWRY'S POINT, DUNNESVILLE, VIRGINIA

City of Anne

For the price of ten thousand pounds of tobacco, anyone could establish a port town in Virginia back in 1680, in accordance with an Act of Assembly at Jamestown. And so the "City of Anne," or Urbanna, was created. The famous Urbanna Oyster Festival, which started in 1957, draws 75,000 visitors every November.

Lowry's Point

The tiny peninsula of Lowry's Point, on the southern Rappahannock River shore, offers fine views of the town of Tappahannock and Downing Bridge. English explorers arrived on the river in 1607 and actively settled here throughout the 18th century.

OPPOSITE: RICHMOND BEACH, TAPPAHANNOCK, VIRGINIA • ABOVE: CROPS ALONG THE RAPPAHANNOCK RIVER

50,000 Farms

Richmond Beach is a residential area located in Essex County along the Rappahannock River. Agriculture has been a major part of Virginia's economy since colonial days. Three centuries later, more than a third of the state remains farmland. Some 50,000 Virginia farms produce hay, soybeans, and corn. Secondary crops include barley, cotton, and tobacco.

OPPOSITE: TAPPAHANNOCK, VIRGINIA • ABOVE: FREDERICKSBURG, VIRGINIA

Oldest Town

Waterfront homes line the bank of the Rappahannock River, on the northern approach to Tappahannock, the oldest town in Essex County. Some historians believe the town may pre-date Williamsburg. Captain John Smith landed here in 1608. Tappahannock means "on the rise and fall of the water" in a local Indian dialect.

Strategic Location

Established in 1671 and named after Prince Frederick, son of King George II, Fredericksburg played a major role during the Civil War. Its strategic location at the falls of the Rappahannock River was bitterly contested by both sides, and several times the city changed hands between the Confederate and Union Armies.

INGLESIDE VINEYARDS, OAK GROVE, VIRGINIA

Wine Country

The climate and soil of Virginia's Northern Neck are similar to those of the Bordeaux region in France, making it ideal for grape cultivation. Several wineries have been established on Northern Neck since the 1970s. The Flemer family's award-winning Ingleside Vineyards, on their 3,000-acre estate, is among Virginia's oldest and largest wineries.

MYER CREEK, CORROTOMAN RIVER, LANCASTER, VIRGINIA

Scenic Waters

Deep, protected waters, beautiful scenery, and a casual atmosphere make the Yankee Point Sailboat Marina popular with boaters from Washington, D.C. and Virginia. It is located on Myer Creek just off the Corrotoman River, 10 miles from the mouth of the Rappahannock River.

TOP : CARTER'S CREEK, RAPPAHANNOCK RIVER, IRVINGTON, VIRGINIA • BOTTOM: MOSQUITO POINT, WHITE STONE, VIRGINIA

Sophisticated Charm

The "Venice of the Northern Neck" at the turn of the 19th century, the busy steamboat port town of Irvington even had its own opera house. Much of the city was consumed by fire in 1917. In 1947, the opening of the Tides Inn began a revitalization of the town, and Irvington once again draws visitors for its relaxed yet sophisticated charm.

Land of Peaceful Living

Native Americans called this area "the land of peaceful living," and the name still holds true. The town of White Stone, settled in 1715, retains its friendly and relaxed attitude. Residents live at an easy pace, guarding their values and traditions. Mosquito Point, at the tip of Virginia's Northern Neck, marks the entrance to the Rappahannock River.

POINT LOOKOUT, CORNFIELD HARBOR, MARYLAND

Marshes and Creeks

Cornfield Harbor is off the beaten path, and that's part of its lure for nature lovers. Located at the mouth of the Potomac River, its access road runs through beautiful marshes and creeks. Its waters produce an abundance of fish, and its sandy banks offer an ideal setting for bird watching and kayaking.

ST. MARY'S GOVERNOR'S CUP YACHT RACE, MARYLAND

Governor's Cup Yacht Race

Each summer, sailors place themselves at the mercy of the unpredictable Chesapeake Bay weather to participate in the largest overnight yacht race on the East Coast. The 70-mile race starts in Annapolis, rain or shine, and finishes the next day at the St. Mary's College waterfront. The awards ceremony and a big party culminate the event.

TOP: POINT LOOKOUT STATE PARK, SCOTLAND, MARYLAND • BOTTOM: TANNER'S CREEK, SCOTLAND BEACH, MARYLAND

Haunted Past

The peaceful setting at Point Lookout State Park makes it hard to imagine that this land once was a prison for more than 50,000 Confederate soldiers, or that its lighthouse is considered one of America's most haunted places. Point Lookout Lighthouse has been the subject of many paranormal investigations.

Tranquil Escape

Quiet and picturesque Scotland Beach is nestled near the southernmost end of St Mary's County, on a peninsula formed by the Potomac River and the Chesapeake Bay. Surrounded by farms and woods, this small community makes a tranquil getaway from city life.

TOP: SOLOMONS ISLAND, MARYLAND • BOTTOM: PATUXENT RIVER, TOWN POINT, MARYLAND

Custom Yacht Fame

Since the late 1800s, Solomons Island has taken full advantage of its position at the mouth of the Patuxent River. A prominent shipbuilding and seafood-harvesting center, the island gained international acclaim in the 1930s as the home of fine wooden yacht builder M.M. Davis & Son. In recent decades, it has become a popular tourist destination.

Thomas Johnson Bridge

Built in 1977 and named after the first governor of Maryland, the graceful 1.5 mile-long Thomas Johnson Bridge connects Solomons Island with St. Mary's County, passing over Town Point and Town Creek. The top of the bridge affords a wonderful view of Solomons Island, the Patuxent River Naval Air Station, and Chesapeake Bay.

SOLOMONS ISLAND AND THOMAS JOHNSON BRIDGE, MARYLAND

Solomons Island

Improved transportation and communications brought tourism to this once-isolated community. Modern hotels and charming B&Bs welcome travelers who come to experience the water-dominant culture. The town offers fishing charters, The Calvert Marine Museum, the wooden-planked Riverwalk boardwalk, and wonderful seafood restaurants.

TOP: FISHING CREEK, CHESAPEAKE BEACH, MARYLAND • BOTTOM: NORTH BEACH, MARYLAND

Railroad Resort Town

In the late 1890s, The Washington and Chesapeake Beach Railway Company envisioned a railroad route from Washington D.C. to a Chesapeake Bay beach. Hence, the resort town of Chesapeake Beach was born. After losing some of its luster in the mid-20th century, the area experienced a revival in the 1990s, and is once again a popular destination.

NORTH BEACH, MARYLAND

Jewel of the Chesapeake

A half-mile boardwalk past homes and shops is dotted with benches providing a vantage point for lovely Chesapeake Bay views. Antiquing and beachcombing are popular pastimes at North Beach, which also is known for its annual summer Bayfest, and a popular house and garden tour. Pretty little North Beach calls itself the Jewel of the Chesapeake.

HOLLAND POINT, ROSE HAVEN, MARYLAND

Holland Point

Stately homes with private boat docks are tucked into the landscape along the waterfront of Holland Point, the southernmost end of Herring Bay. Holland Point overlooks both Herring Bay and the Chesapeake Bay. Minutes away are Herrington Harbour and the towns of North Beach and Chesapeake Beach.

HERRINGTON HARBOUR, ROSE HAVEN, MARYLAND

World Class Marinas

Herrington Harbour was created in the late 1970s when visionary E. Steuart Chaney embarked on a mission to create an environmentally-friendly waterfront development. Owned and operated by the Chaney family, Herrington Harbour encompasses two marinas, an inn, a restaurant, an Olympic pool, and a Caribbean-style beachfront.

HERRING BAY, FAIRHAVEN-ON-THE-BAY, MARYLAND

Once an Oyster Bar

In the 1850s, large oyster bars attracted watermen from the Eastern Shore to Herring Bay. One of them, Bay Shore Bar, extended from Herring Bay to West River. Gradually, people from the cities migrated into the area for sport fishing and relaxation. Now, Fairhaven-on-the-Bay features magazine-cover homes along its picturesque banks.

DEALE, MARYLAND

Fishing and Boating

Deale, Maryland is very serious about its fishing and boating. In addition to several smaller marinas, there are two large full-service marinas, Shipwright Harbor and Herrington Harbor North. Home to over 40 charter fishing boats, Deale provides easy access to the Chesapeake Bay for the residents of the Washington, D.C. and Annapolis areas.

PARKER CREEK, REST HAVEN, DEALE, MARYLAND

Luxury Homes

Less than a century ago, the residential community of Rest Haven was primarily farmland. Now, the lovely peninsula east of Deale, bordered by Parker Creek and Deale Beach, is graced by large waterfront houses.

PARRISH CREEK, SHADY SIDE, MARYLAND

Preserving Culture

The small town of Shady Side, on the peninsula between the Chesapeake Bay and the West River, takes pride in preserving its history and folklore for future generations. The Maryland town is home to The Captain Salem Avery House Museum, run by the Shady Side Rural Heritage Society.

OPPOSITE: PARRISH CREEK, SHADY SIDE, MARYLAND • ABOVE: WEST RIVER, GALESVILLE, MARYLAND

Watermen's Town

Visible here from the air are Shady Side Marina and Discovery Village eco-park, on Parrish Creek. Discovery Village is a research and educational facility dedicated to preserving the ecology and culture of the Chesapeake Bay. It is currently working together with the Chesapeake Bay Foundation on an oyster restoration project.

Sailing Town

The town of Galesville, on the West River, once was the terminus of a steamship line connecting to Annapolis and Baltimore. From a thriving community of Chesapeake Bay watermen, the town has developed its industry around pleasure boating. Today, Galesville is home to the West River Sailing Club, one of the most active sailing clubs on the bay.

BEVERLY BEACH, MARYLAND

Quiet Community

Despite its close proximity to major cities like Washington, D.C. and Baltimore, Beverly Beach remains quiet and modest. It is a small private residential community, which consists of approximately 400 homes, a private beach, and a marina. The adjacent Beverly Triton Beach Park is a nature preserve with three ponds and wetlands.

SOUTH RIVER, SAUNDERS POINT, MARYLAND

Mayo Beach

Homeowners on Saunders Point, at the mouth of the South River, have both choices: a tranquil evening on their porch overlooking the bay, or an easy boat ride to Kent Island or Annapolis for a fine meal and cultural entertainment. The adjacent Mayo Beach Park offers picnicking, swimming, and other recreational activities.

SHOREHAM BEACH, MARYLAND

Pretty Town

Shoreham Beach, at the entrance to the South River, offers the best of both water and land. Mature trees line the streets and beaches beckon for a lunch *en plein air*, while the river and the bay lure enthusiastic boaters. Ramsay Lake and Selby Bay, visible in the distance, have several marinas.

SOUTH RIVER, TURKEY POINT, MARYLAND

Turkey Point

Sandwiched between Ramsay Lake (visible on the left) and Selby Bay (on the right), near the mouth of South River, is the community of Turkey Point. It was established on two connected islands with the fitting names of Big Island and Little Island. The three bodies of water surrounding Turkey Point offer endless recreational possibilities.

SOUTH RIVER, CAPE LOCH HAVEN, MARYLAND

Quiet and Green

Cape Loch Haven lies just down the river from London Town. Currently an archeological site for studies by The Lost Towns Project, London Town once was a prosperous tobacco port that rivaled the colonial capitals of Williamsburg and Annapolis. Quiet and green, Cape Loch Haven's historic London Town House and Gardens are well worth a visit.

BACK CREEK, EASTPORT, THE SPA CREEK, AND THE SEVREN RIVER, ANNAPOLIS, MARYLAND

America's First Colonial Capital

First established in 1649 as the settlement of Providence, the Puritan settlement of Annapolis was chosen as Colonial Maryland's capital in 1694. The Royal Governor named this new seat of power after Princess Anne, an heiress to the British throne. It attracted much cultural and maritime activity and quickly became a fashionable metropolis of Colonial America.

SPA CREEK, ANNAPOLIS, MARYLAND

Georgian Architecture

In the early 18th century, prosperous merchants built their Georgian townhouses near the water. Annapolis has the greatest concentration of 18th-century Georgian architecture in America. All four of Maryland's signers of the Declaration of Independence lived in Annapolis, and three of their homes are open for public touring.

SPA CREEK, ANNAPOLIS, MARYLAND

Spa Creek

The Naval Academy, the Annapolis Sailing School, and hundreds of recreational boaters keep the Annapolis harbor busy. Thousands of small vessels pass through Spa Creek every year. Its nearly equidistant location between Washington, D.C. and Baltimore makes Annapolis a convenient, popular, and delightful destination for residents from both cities.

SPA CREEK BRIDGE, SPA CREEK, ANNAPOLIS, MARYLAND

Yachting Fame

The internationally-renowned Annapolis Yacht Club began in 1883 as an informal canoe club. It now has more than 1400 members and fleets on both sides of Spa Creek. Nearby is the City Dock, in the heart of historic Annapolis. Major maritime attractions include the springtime Maritime Heritage Festival, boat shows, and waterfront dining.

SPA CREEK DRAW BRIDGE, ANNAPOLIS, MARYLAND

America's Sailing Capital

Annapolis and its surrounding county embrace nearly 400 miles of the bay and its tributaries, making it the seat of sailing power on the Chesapeake Bay. On breezy summer days, the waterways are dotted with sailboats of all sizes, racing in the wind or cruising at a leisurely pace.

MARYLAND STATEHOUSE AND DOWNTOWN ANNAPOLIS, MARYLAND

Oldest State House

The Maryland State House is the oldest state house still in legislative use. It served as the United States Capitol from 1783 to 1784. The Maryland General Assembly convenes there for three months each year. The original building was completed in 1779, the Dome in 1797. The Dome is thought to have been modeled after a tower in Karlsruhe, Germany.

ABOVE: NAVY-MARINE CORPS MEMORIAL STADIUM, ANNAPOLIS, MARYLAND • PAGES 66–67: U.S. NAVAL ACADEMY, ANNAPOLIS, MARYLAND

Packed Houses

There is no lack of spectators any time of year at this stadium. The games played by the Navy Midshipmen in this 34,000-seat facility since its dedication in 1959 have attracted more than 4 million fans. The stadium was completely renovated in 2004 and transformed into a state-of-the-art multi-use facility hosting Navy football, lacrosse, and other events.

United States Naval Academy

The United States Naval Academy is an undergraduate institution that prepares young men and women to become fully commissioned naval and marine officers. Since its founding in 1845, more than 60,000 have successfully completed the program. Thousands of proud parents arrive on campus every May for the midshipmen's graduation.

TOP: MILL CREEK, MARYLAND • BOTTOM: CHESAPEAKE BAY, OPEN WATERS

SANDY POINT STATE PARK, ANNAPOLIS, MARYLAND

Jet Skiing on Mill Creek

An aerial shot gives a bird's-eye perspective of jet skiers on Mill Creek, near Hidden Point, just north of Annapolis. Hidden Point, once mostly farmland, now boasts waterfront homes, the Chesapeake Bay Institute Field Laboratory of Johns Hopkins University, and the U.S. Naval Ship Research and Development Center at Greenbury Point.

Amazing Schooner Race

One of the world's largest and most impressive gatherings of traditional sailing vessels, The Great Chesapeake Bay Schooner Race is an annual sailing race from Baltimore to Portsmouth to benefit the Chesapeake Bay Foundation and the Elizabeth River Project. The public can view the fleet of magnificent schooners during their stay in either port.

Bay Views

Sandy Point State Park affords excellent views of the Chesapeake Bay and bridge. Opened in 1952, its 786 acres are rich with wildlife and recreational opportunities such as swimming, crabbing, boating, and windsurfing. Visitors can enjoy a summer picnic while watching ship and boat traffic on the bay.

OPPOSITE: SANDY POINT SHOAL LIGHT, SKIDMORE, MARYLAND • ABOVE: CHESAPEAKE BAY BRIDGE, MARYLAND

Victorian Elegance

Sandy Point Shoal Light features a copper roof made white with sea salt. It has a black lantern and an octagonal appearance due to its truncated corners. The mansard roof, peaked windows, bracketed cornices, and ornamental brickwork give it an unusual Victorian style and elegance. It was auctioned off in 2006 and is now privately owned.

Chesapeake Bay Bridge

With a shore-to-shore length of 4.3 miles, the Chesapeake Bay Bridge is among the world's most dramatic over-water structures. The two-lane original span was opened to traffic in 1952; the parallel structure opened in 1973. Both spans have a vertical navigational clearance of 186 feet, which allows the passage of ships to and from the Port of Baltimore.

ABOVE AND OPPOSITE: CHESAPEAKE BAY BRIDGE, MARYLAND

25 Million Vehicles

The Chesapeake Bay Bridge replaced the need for ferries from the Annapolis area to the Eastern Shore. Now, nearly 25 million vehicles annually cross the bridge to ocean resorts and quaint historic towns. Since its construction, the bridge has made significant impact on both sides of the bay, especially on the growth of Eastern Shore communities.

Volvo Ocean Race

The Volvo Ocean Race is a major yacht race around the world. Originally called the Whitbread Round the World Yacht Race, it was conceived by the Royal Naval Sailing Association in 1973, with sponsorship from a London-based brewery company, and was the first ever attempt at a global, crewed yacht race. The race covers more than 28,000 miles.

BAYSIDE BEACH, BODKIN CREEK, PASADENA, MARYLAND

Historic Park

Waterfront homes and boats dot the shorelines of Bayside Beach on secluded Bodkin Creek. At the historic Hancock's Resolution Park on Bayside Beach stands a pre-Civil War stone farmhouse. This is an excellent example of early Chesapeake architecture. Boyd Pond, Fort Smallwood Park, and Rock Creek are visible in the background.

TOP: STONY CREEK, MARYLAND • BOTTOM: FRANCIS SCOTT KEY BRIDGE, BALTIMORE HARBOR, MARYLAND

Stony Creek

Peaceful residential communities have replaced the batteries and fire towers that served as coastal defenses along Stony Creek in the 19th and early 20th centuries. Today's recreational boats and waterfront homes are pictured here, counterclockwise, on Stony Beach, Orchard Beach, Clearwater Beach, Sunset Beach, and Riviera Beach.

O Say Can You See?

Arching dramatically over Baltimore Harbor, and reaching the height of a 36-story building, the 1.6-mile Francis Scott Key Bridge crosses the Patapsco River from Hawkins Point to Sollers Point. The bridge is a part of the 11-mile-long Outer Harbor Crossing toll facility, which accommodates about 31,000 vehicles a day. The bridge affords a view of the site of the 1812 bombardment of Fort McHenry, the battle that inspired Key to write *The Star Spangled Banner.*

FORT MCHENRY, ENTRANCE TO BALTIMORE HARBOR, MARYLAND

Baltimore Harbor

Star-shaped Fort McHenry stands guard at the entrance to Baltimore Harbor. Baltimore is an important international seaport, Maryland's largest city, and home to Johns Hopkins University. Baltimore's Inner Harbor area has a vibrant mix of restaurants, entertainment, historic ships, museums, sports complexes, and more.

TOP: SEVEN FOOT KNOLL LIGHTHOUSE, BALTIMORE MARITIME MUSEUM • BOTTOM: INNER HARBOR, BALTIMORE, MARYLAND • OPPOSITE: PRIDE OF BALTIMORE II

Oldest Screw-pile Lighthouse

The Chesapeake Bay's oldest surviving screw-pile lighthouse was built in 1855 at the mouth of the Patapsco River as an aid to navigation. One hundred and thirty-three years later, the Coast Guard donated the lighthouse to the City of Baltimore to be preserved as an historic landmark. It is now part of the Baltimore Maritime Museum.

USS Constellation

The USS *Constellation*, built in 1854, was the last all-sail warship built by the United States Navy. It served in the Civil War and also for training, diplomatic, and humanitarian purposes. Today, it is a National Historic Landmark, open for tours. Rising behind the ship is Baltimore's World Trade Center, the world's tallest equilateral five-sided building.

Pride of Baltimore II

In 1977, the City of Baltimore launched the *Pride of Baltimore*, an authentic reproduction of an early 19th-century Clipper privateer. Lost at sea after nine years of service and 150,000 nautical miles, she was replaced by a modern *Pride of Baltimore II* in 1988. The *Pride* continues the role of Maryland's Flagship and Goodwill Ambassador.

PRIDE OF BALTIMORE II
BALTIMORE
MARYLAND

TOP: OLD ROAD BAY, NORTH POINT, PATAPSCO RIVER, FORT HOWARD, MARYLAND • BOTTOM: OLD ROAD BAY, EDGEMERE, MARYLAND

Fort Howard

Known as The Bulldog at Baltimore's Gate, Fort Howard was created to protect the valued Port of Baltimore. It served its purpose in 1814, when the Americans slowed down the advance of the British troops in the Battle of North Point. Today, Fort Howard is a public park, where many of its batteries can still be seen.

Edge of the Sea

The township of Edgemere, Old English for "edge of the sea," is the largest community on the North Point Peninsula of Baltimore County, accessible via the Baltimore Beltway, the Patapsco River, and the Chesapeake Bay.

SWAN POINT, NORTH POINT STATE PARK, BACK RIVER, EDGEMERE, MARYLAND

Swan Point

Clusters of homes and a marina nestle on this swan's neck-shaped peninsula at the entrance to the Back River. Its proximity to Baltimore makes Swan Point a coveted waterfront community. North Point is a state park with rich history, from a defense against the British in 1812 to a large amusement park in the first half of the 20th century. Its amenities include horseback and hiking trails, boat launches, camping, picnicking, and a comprehensive visitor center.

TOP: MIDDLE RIVER AND ESSEX SUBURBS, MARYLAND • BOTTOM: ENTRANCE TO SUSQUEHANNA RIVER, HAVRE DE GRACE, MARYLAND
OPPOSITE: THOMAS J HATEM MEMORIAL BRIDGE, SUSQUEHANNA RIVER, HAVRE DE GRACE, MARYLAND

Waterfront Communities

In 1929, Glenn L. Martin built an airplane factory in Middle River. By the 1940s, thousands were employed at the factory, now Lockheed Martin. Since then, increased interest in waterfront homes inspired some of the county's most desirable communities, including Island View Beach, Breezy Point Beach, Rockaway Beach, and Cape May Beach.

Millard E. Tydings Memorial Park

Honoring Havre de Grace's most famous native son, United States Senator Millard E. Tydings, this beautiful park affords magnificent views of the Susquehanna River. Along the water's edge is the city's yacht basin. The park hosts many events, including Memorial Day services, Fourth of July fireworks, arts and crafts shows, and the annual seafood festival.

Havre de Grace

Named after the port city of Le Havre, France, Havre de Grace is very popular for water recreation. Dotting the shoreline are a city yacht basin and several marinas. The waterfront promenade is perfect for a relaxing stroll on a calm summer evening. Havre de Grace missed becoming our nation's capital by just one vote.

HAVRE DE GRACE QUARRY, SUSQUEHANNA RIVER, HAVRE DE GRACE, MARYLAND

Aggregate Quarries

Aggregate rock, from quarries like this one, is barged all over the country. Aggregates form the foundation of many great buildings, bridges, highways, and airport runways. A very large aggregate quarry can yield as much as 10 million tons of rock per year, enough to fill 10,000 rail cars.

THOMAS J. HATEM MEMORIAL BRIDGE, SUSQUEHANNA RIVER, PERRYVILLE, MARYLAND

Thomas J. Hatem Memorial Bridge

More than 200 bridges cross the Susquehanna, which at 444 miles long, is the longest river on America's East Coast. Formed from two branches, one in upstate New York and the other in western Pennsylvania, it provides half of the freshwater inflow for the entire Chesapeake Bay. The Thomas J. Hatem Memorial Bridge connects Havre de Grace and Perryville.

TOP: NORTH EAST RIVER, CHARLESTOWN, MARYLAND • BOTTOM: ELK RIVER, LOCUST POINT, ELKTON, MARYLAND • OPPOSITE: SUMMIT NORTH MARINA, C&D CANAL, BEAR, DELAWARE

Charlestown

Charlestown (Charles Town) was established by a 1742 Act of the Maryland Assembly to encourage trade in the northern Chesapeake Bay. A major supply depot for the Continental Army during the Revolutionary War, the town witnessed two encounters with British warships. Today, Charlestown is a quiet community, with a well-preserved historic district.

Locust Point

Located at the northeastern shore of the Elk River and near the bustling city of Elkton, Locust Point offers scenic views from both land and water. Elk Neck State Park, the C&D Canal, and Welch Point Wildlife Management Area are easily accessible by boat from Locust Point and Taylors Island marinas.

Chesapeake-Delaware Canal

The C&D Canal, connecting the Delaware River with the Chesapeake Bay, is one of only two commercially vital sea-level canals in the United States. It is 14 miles long, 450 feet wide and 35 feet deep. The C&D Canal is owned and operated by the United States Army Corps of Engineers.

SENATOR WILLIAM V. ROTH, JR. BRIDGE AND ST. GEORGES BRIDGE, CHESAPEAKE-DELAWARE CANAL, ST. GEORGES, MARYLAND

Shipping Traffic

The value of connecting the northern Chesapeake Bay with the Delaware River was recognized as early as the 17th century; however, the first waterway was not open for business until 1829. Today's canal is a modern, electronically-controlled commercial waterway, carrying 40 percent of all ship traffic in and out of the Port of Baltimore.

TOP: SASSAFRAS RIVER, GEORGETOWN AND FREDERICKTOWN, MARYLAND • BOTTOM: GROVE NECK AND SASSAFRAS RIVER, MARYLAND

Sassafras River Drawbridge

This 5-foot high bascule bridge connects the Maryland towns of Georgetown on the southern shore to Fredericktown, on the northern shore. The brother villages were named for the sons of King George III. Ideal ways to pass the day in this part of the Chesapeake Bay would include crabbing along the river and poking through antique shops.

Between the Rivers

Grove Point on Grove Neck is located between the mouths of the Elk and the Sassafras rivers and marks the southeastern border of Cecil County. A small pond near the tip of Grove Neck neighbors Cheshaven, a small community 31 miles to the east of Baltimore.

TOP: SASSAFRAS RIVER, BETTERTON, MARYLAND • BOTTOM: GREAT OAK LANDING, FAIRLEE CREEK, CHESTERTOWN, MARYLAND • OPPOSITE: WORTON CREEK, CHESTERTOWN, MARYLAND

Popular Beach

Overlooking the confluence of the Sassafras, Elk, and Susquehanna rivers, Betterton was founded as a fishing village in the mid-1700s. A century later, the development of steamboats made Betterton ideally situated as a port and, later, as a thriving summer resort. Betterton today is a quiet residential community with a sandy beach favored by swimmers.

Luxury Resort

Beautifully positioned on Fairlee Creek overlooking the upper Chesapeake Bay, Mears Great Oak Landing is a 70-acre, 350-slip full-service resort marina. Established in 1955 as a private yacht club, marina, and hunting lodge, it grew into a large enterprise featuring a restaurant, lodge, banquet facilities, golf course, tropical bar, and other amenities.

Tranquil Marina

Worton Creek, in Kent County, Maryland, is part of the Upper Eastern Shore Tributary Basin. The creek is 2.5 miles long, with headwaters near Worton Park. It hosts the full-service, 100-slip Worton Creek Marina.

ROCK HALL, MARYLAND

Preserving the Culture

Rock Hall traces its history to 1707, as an important tobacco port and a fishing, crabbing, and oystering center. Today, Rock Hall preserves the watermen's culture while providing travelers with an alluring destination for sailing and boating, art, festivals, and seafood restaurants.

TOLCHESTER BEACH, MARYLAND

Tolchester Marina

For 85 years, Tolchester Beach was home to an amusement park, which grew from a modest 10 acres in 1877 to a flourishing 155-acre attraction that drew 20,000 visitors a weekend. The amusement park closed in 1962. Tolchester Marina is a full service marina.

CHESTERTOWN, MARYLAND

Royal Port of Entry

Founded in 1706, Chestertown was one of the colony's six Royal Ports of Entry. By the mid-18th century, it trailed only Annapolis as a leading port. Today, it is a quaint and lovely town with stately historic homes, small shops, excellent restaurants, and stunning views from the town dock. Chestertown also is home to Washington College.

TOP: TILGHMAN CREEK ENTERING CHESTER RIVER, MARYLAND • BOTTOM: QUEENSTOWN AND QUEENSTOWN CREEK, MARYLAND

Tea Party Site

The Chester River, 40 miles long, is a major tributary of the Chesapeake Bay. In the 18th and 19th centuries, it played an important role in Maryland's economy. In 1774, Chestertown mimicked the Boston Tea Party with its own tea party on the Chester River. The river now provides pleasure to recreational boaters and sailors.

Queenstown

Named after Queen Anne of England, Queenstown celebrated its 300th anniversary in 2007. The town has the oldest continuously-used courthouse in the state. From its steamboat-based economy of the 1850s, it has evolved as a center of agriculture and seafood harvesting. It also boasts retail shopping outlets and the Queenstown Harbor Lake Golf Course.

QUEEN'S LANDING, CHESTER, MARYLAND

Queen's Landing

In the Northern part of Chester is Queen's Landing, a condominium complex that offers its residents beautiful marina views of Macum Creek and expansive vistas of the Chester River right from a living room or a screened porch.

TOP AND BOTTOM: GRASONVILLE, EAST TO KENT ISLAND, MARYLAND

The Narrows

Kent Narrows is the name for both the water passage that separates Kent Island from the Delmarva Peninsula and the community through which it runs. Each year, nearly 30 million drivers cross the Route 50 Kent Narrows Bridge on their way to the Atlantic Ocean beaches. In recent decades, Kent Narrows has seen rapid growth of waterfront townhouses, condos, hotels, marinas, and restaurants. On weekends, the Narrows is alive with beach commuters and boaters visiting local restaurants and waterfront bars. Despite the growth, several large seafood packinghouses remain, clustered around Kent Narrows; and watermen still ply the bay in their age-old quest for blue crabs and soft-shell clams.

LOVE POINT, KENT ISLAND, MARYLAND

Love Point

Love Point is the northernmost tip of Kent Island. As boaters round Love Point heading southeast, they may choose to head up the Chester River toward Chestertown for a leisurely afternoon trip or to make a straight shot to the Kent Narrows, several miles to the south.

THOMPSON CREEK, KENT ISLAND, MARYLAND

Quintessential Kent Island

Waterfront homes and their private docks line Thompson Creek as it winds its way southbound to the Eastern Bay. The visual contrast between the waterfront homes and the surrounding farmers' fields is a quintessential Kent Island landscape.

TOP: BAY BRIDGE MARINA, STEVENSVILLE, MARYLAND • BOTTOM: QUEEN ANNE MARINA, STEVENSVILLE, MARYLAND • OPPOSITE: GATEWAY MARINA, TRAPPE, MARYLAND

Marinas of Kent Island

Kent Island is less than an hour's drive from the Baltimore and Washington Beltways. The many marinas afford boating opportunities for those who want to escape the city for a more bucolic Chesapeake Bay lifestyle. Gateway Marina is one of the few marinas with direct bay access. There are many others that face secluded bays, rivers, and creeks.

TOWER GARDEN ON THE BAY, KENT ISLAND, MARYLAND

Upscale Getaways

During the mid-20th century, local working people built modest homes on Kent Island. In recent years, wealthy mid-Atlantic residents have discovered the charms of Kent Island, and have replaced the original bungalows with large modern homes for use as weekend getaways.

KENT POINT, KENT ISLAND, MARYLAND

Kent Point Marina

Positioned at Kent Island's southernmost point, Kent Point Marina affords easy access for boating on the Chesapeake Bay, the Eastern Bay, and their tributaries.

EASTERN COX NECK, KENT ISLAND, MARYLAND

Kent Island

Residents at the narrowest part of Eastern Cox Neck, a peninsula in the south of Kent Island, have a superb vantage point to enjoy the sunsets over Cox Creek and other southern Kent Island peninsulas to the west.

NORMANS POINT, CRAB ALLEY NECK, CRAB ALLEY BAY, DOMINION, KENT ISLAND, MARYLAND

Crab Alley Neck

Sandwiched between Crab Alley Bay and Prospect Bay is claw-shaped Crab Alley Neck and its most southern tip, Norman's Point. The waters on the southeastern shore of Kent Island have been teeming with blue crabs for centuries, aptly earning its name. Families enjoy crabbing right off their private docks. The time-tested method to catch a crab is to tie a chicken neck to the end of a string, gently pull the tenacious decapods to the surface, and then swiftly scoop them up with a net.

RESTAURANT & BAR

OPPOSITE, TOP: ROUTE 50 BLUE STAR MEMORIAL HWY, KENT ISLAND AND KENT NARROWS, MARYLAND • OPPOSITE, BOTTOM: KENT NARROWS, GRASONVILLE, MARYLAND
ABOVE: CHESAPEAKE BAY CRABS

Blue Star Memorial Highway

U.S. Route 50 traverses the state of Maryland, connecting Washington, D.C. with Ocean City on Maryland's Atlantic shore. After passing Annapolis, it becomes the Blue Star Memorial Highway, a designation that pays tribute to the armed forces of World War II. Both roadways depend on the Chesapeake Bay Bridge to reach Kent Island from Sandy Point State Park.

Fisherman's Crab Deck

A true local institution, Fisherman's Crab Deck on Kent Narrows dates back to 1930, when Captain Alex Thomas and his wife opened the original Fisherman's Inn with seating for 30. Now an Eastern Shore landmark, the family-owned and operated Fisherman's Village comprises an inn, a seafood market, and a crab deck.

Chesapeake Bounty

The ubiquitous blue crab, which turns red when steamed, is the icon of summertime on the Chesapeake Bay. Whether served up steamed on a newspaper-covered table, or combined with other ingredients into a favorite crab dish, they're a delicious element of Chesapeake Bay life.

TOP: OYSTER COVE, GRASONVILLE, MARYLAND • BOTTOM: PINEY NECK POINT, GRASONVILLE, MARYLAND

Balance of Nature

Oyster Cove is a modern community surrounded by Marshy Creek and Prospect Bay. Condominiums and townhouses were artfully designed to blend into the natural beauty of the peninsula. The architects took care to protect the shore's delicate ecologic balance, while accommodating the need for the conveniences of contemporary waterfront living.

Piney Neck Point

One of Chesapeake Bay's legendary sunsets illuminates the grand houses on Piney Neck Point, between Eastern Bay and Greenwood Creek. Eastern Bay is a tributary of the Chesapeake Bay and is located south of the Chester River and north of the Choptank River. It is connected to the Chester River via Kent Narrows.

WYE RIVER, BENNETT POINT LIGHTHOUSE, GRASONVILLE, MARYLAND

Mouth of the Wye

An intriguing private lighthouse on the tip of Bennett Point marks the mouth of the Wye River. The Wye River is popular with recreational boaters for its beautiful secluded anchorages, fishing, crabbing, and proximity to tourist attractions. The river's most notable feature is the Wye Island Natural Resources Management Area.

MILES RIVER, MARYLAND

Twilight on the Tributary

All is quiet at twilight on the Miles River. The boats are resting after a day's work or recreational sailing on the river, and nature is getting ready for the night. A tributary of the Eastern Bay traveling from Unionville to the east, Miles River is part of the Chesapeake Bay watershed.

HAMBLETON COVE AND PORTER CREEK, ST. MICHAELS, MARYLAND

Harbourtowne Golf Resort

The town of St. Michaels is home to the 153-acre Harbourtowne Golf Resort and Conference Center. It features breathtaking waterfront views and a Pete Dye-designed golf course with his trademark narrow fairways and deep traps, ponds, walls, and protected greens.

ST. MICHAELS, MARYLAND

Trendy St. Michaels

Founded in 1677, St. Michaels was a shipbuilding center and a trading port until the early 1800s. It is known as "the town that fooled the British" because of a clever defense strategy during the War of 1812. Today, it is a trendy destination with upscale shops and restaurants. The movie *Wedding Crashers* was filmed in St. Michaels in 2004.

TOP: THE INN AT PERRY CABIN, MILES RIVER, ST. MICHAELS, MARYLAND • BOTTOM: MILES RIVER, ST. MICHAELS, MARYLAND

The Inn at Perry Cabin

The luxurious Inn at Perry Cabin is a tranquil and refined respite for visitors from nearby Washington, D.C., Baltimore or locations beyond. Built after the War of 1812, the country house became an inn in 1990. Its cuisine is famous throughout the area.

Crabbing on the Chesapeake

Trotline fishing, one of many crabbing methods, is mostly employed by commercial fishermen such as this one. A baited line, weighted to the bottom, allows the crabber to net the busily-feeding crabs as the line rises to the surface.

TOP: RICH NECK, CLAIBORNE, MARYLAND • BOTTOM: NAVY POINT, ST. MICHAELS, MARYLAND • OPPOSITE: EASTERN BAY SHORELINE, WITTMAN, MARYLAND

Claiborne

Claiborne was a busy port, first for passenger and then automobile ferry service across the Chesapeake Bay from 1890 and until 1952. Claiborne is home to Rich Neck Manor, granted to James Mitchell in 1652, later property of Matthew and Lloyd Tilghman. Jolly Sam, the Christmas pony, now resides in Mineral Spring Farm, in Claiborne.

Chesapeake Bay Maritime Museum

Founded in 1965, the Chesapeake Bay Maritime Museum promotes the appreciation of culture and maritime heritage of the Chesapeake Bay. The museum is housed in the Hooper Strait Lighthouse, which was saved from demolition and barged 60 miles to the site. Besides traditional exhibits, the museum offers unique interactive programs.

Wittman

A magnificent shoreline estate faces the open waters of Eastern Bay in Wittman, Talbot County, Maryland. Wittman is a community between St. Michaels and Tilghman Island, and a short driving distance from Easton. Talbot County is a choice destination for sailors, antique shoppers, hunters, fishermen, and history buffs.

TOP: TILGHMAN ISLAND, KNAPPS NARROWS, MARYLAND • BOTTOM: HARRIS CREEK, TILGHMAN ISLAND, MARYLAND; CHESAPEAKE BAY IN THE DISTANCE

Knapp's Narrows Drawbridge

The Knapp's Narrows drawbridge, connecting Tilghman Island to the mainland, is one of the most active drawbridges in the world. It opens between 10,000 and 15,000 times per year. The current bridge replaced an earlier structure in 1998; the former bridge now serves as the entrance to the Chesapeake Bay Maritime Museum in St. Michael's.

Tilghman Island

Three-mile-long Tilghman Island was first charted by Captain John Smith in 1608. Since the late 19th century, the island has been a popular haven for vacationers drawn by superb water activities and genteel accommodations. Bird watching, sailing, paddling and boating, as well as sport fishing and hunting are the most popular outdoor recreational activities. The island is home to the only commercial sailing fleet in North America, the Chesapeake Bay Skipjacks.

BLACK WALNUT COVE, BLACK WALNUT POINT, TILGHMAN ISLAND, MARYLAND

Idyllic Setting

Fifty-seven acres of a wildlife preserve on the southernmost tip of Tilghman Island offer beautiful water views and waterfowl-watching at the Black Walnut Point Bed & Breakfast Inn, where guests also can admire sunrises over the Choptank River and sunsets over the Chesapeake Bay.

OPPOSITE: EDGE CREEK, ROYAL OAK, MARYLAND • TOP AND BOTTOM: PLAIN DEALING CREEK AND TAR CREEK, BELLEVIEW, MARYLAND

Prime Real Estate

Edge Creek takes its name from James Edge, who in 1755 owned more than 700 acres of surrounding land. Edge Creek is a tributary of Broad Creek, which is in turn a tributary of the Choptank River. Located halfway between St. Michaels and Oxford and not far from Easton, Edge Creek is considered prime waterfront real estate.

Sister Creeks

Spacious waterfront homes offer a tranquil atmosphere and beautiful views from the banks of Tar Creek and Plain Dealing Creek, small tributaries of the Tred Avon River in Talbot County, Maryland. The sister creeks are just east-northeast of Bellevue and opposite the historic town of Oxford.

TRED AVON RIVER, BELLEVUE, MARYLAND

Oldest Ferry

The Oxford-Bellevue Ferry, believed to be the nation's oldest privately operated ferry, started in 1683. Service was discontinued after the American Revolution, resumed in 1836, and has been in operation since. The 20-minute round-trip service crosses the Tred Avon River between Oxford and Bellevue and can accommodate up to nine cars.

TOP AND BOTTOM: TOWN CREEK, TRED AVON RIVER, OXFORD, MARYLAND

Oxford

Established in 1683, Oxford is among Maryland's oldest towns. Located near the mouth of the Tred Avon River and surrounded by wealthy tobacco plantations, Oxford flourished as an international port until the American Revolution. Today, it is a waterman's town that also enjoys a growing tourism and leisure economy. Its quiet charm, fresh air, and clean water provide a haven from the hustle and bustle of city life for boaters, weekend visitors, and summer residents.

PIER STREET MARINA, OXFORD, MARYLAND

Pier Street Marina

Located in the southern part of Historic Oxford, Maryland, with westerly views of the Tred Avon and Choptank rivers, is the 62-slip Pier Street Marina. Tourists and locals can dock their boats and watch the river activities, while feasting on crabs and homemade pies at The Masthead Restaurant.

BACHELORS POINT, OXFORD, MARYLAND

Campbell's Bachelor Point Yacht Co.

This 80-slip marina at the mouth of the Tred Avon River is surrounded by fourteen serene acres, twelve of which are a wildlife sanctuary. Campbell's Bachelor Point Yacht Company specializes in the building and restoration of quality custom boats, from cocktail cruisers to luxury yachts.

ENTRANCE TO ISLAND CREEK, CHOPTANK RIVER, OXFORD, MARYLAND

Island Creek

Just south of Oxford, Maryland, Island Creek is a peaceful inlet off the Choptank River. Nestled among magnolias and willows on the banks of the creek is the elegant Combsberry Bed and Breakfast, a country manor which once was an Eastern Shore plantation. Autumn boaters may want to have cameras ready for the beautiful colors and migrating birds.

LA TRAPPE CREEK, TRAPPE, MARYLAND

LaTrappe Creek

Martin Point marks the entrance to La Trappe Creek, a tributary of the Lower Choptank River in Talbot County, Maryland. La Trappe is a lovely destination for a short weekend trip from anywhere in the bay. It is quiet and semi-sheltered and is a showcase for beautiful sunsets.

CHOPTANK RIVER, CAMBRIDGE, MARYLAND

Long Wharf Park

At the end of High Street in Cambridge, Long Wharf Park offers public waterfront access to the Choptank riverbank. Residents and visitors enjoy fishing, picnics, and educational cruises on the skipjack *Nathan of Dorchester*. Cambridge Creek and Senator Frederick C. Malkus Bridge are visible in the background.

HYATT REGENCY CHESAPEAKE BAY GOLF RESORT, SPA, AND MARINA, CAMBRIDGE, MARYLAND

Popular Resort

The 400-acre Hyatt Regency Chesapeake Bay Golf Resort, Spa and Marina opened in 2002 as the first destination resort in the Cambridge area. The resort, on the banks of the Choptank River, is popular for meetings, family reunions, and vacation getaways.

ABOVE: WARWICK RIVER, SECRETARY, MARYLAND • OPPOSITE: CAMBRIDGE, MARYLAND

Quiet Village

Secretary, a quiet village in the Cambridge metro area along the Warwick River, was named for Henry Sewell, secretary of the colony under Governor Charles Calvert in the late 17th century. Secretary and its neighboring town, Hurlock, are connected by the infamous Suicide Bridge.

Cambridge

Its location on the southern bank of the Choptank River makes Cambridge one of the most charming settings on the Eastern Shore. The city is praised for its lovely shaded streets and beautiful Victorian homes. Established in 1684, Cambridge is one of the oldest towns in Maryland, with a rich maritime and cultural heritage.

ABOVE: WRIGHTS CREEK, CHOPTANK RIVER, CAMBRIDGE, MARYLAND • OPPOSITE: NANTICOKE, MARYLAND

Oyster Shell Point

Homes dot the lush green countryside on the banks of the Choptank River and Wrights Creek just east of Cambridge, Maryland. The residents of Oyster Shell Point enjoy both the pleasures of tranquil living on the waterfront, and the conveniences of nearby towns.

Roaring Point

An elegant line of sand marks Roaring Point in Nanticoke. A nearby waterfront campground offers a peaceful retreat with views of the Nanticoke River and Tangier Sound. Nanticoke Harbor, which accommodates a variety of small vessels, is visible on the right. Many cruisers consider the Nanticoke River the most beautiful tributary of the Chesapeake Bay.

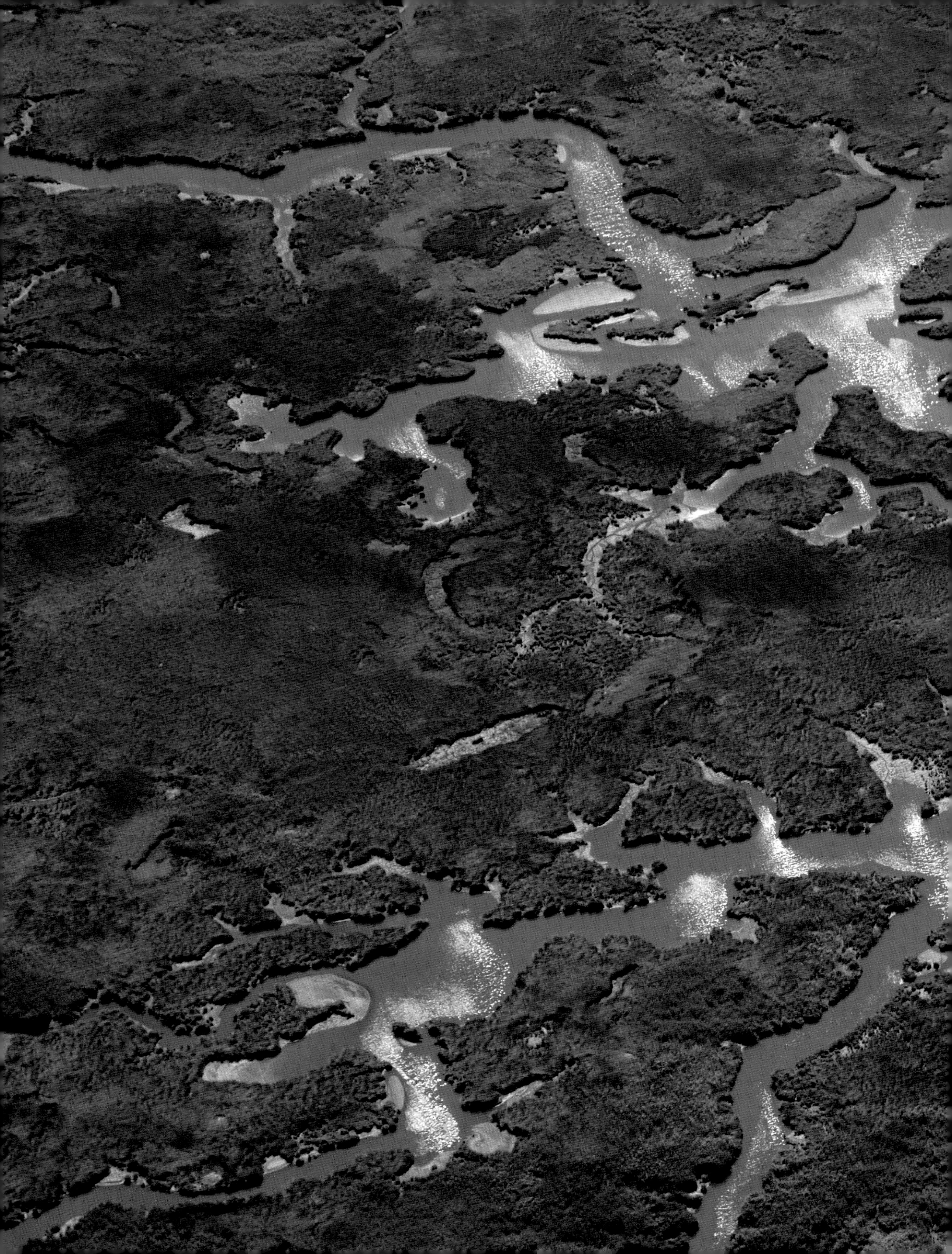

PAGES 134–135: BLACKWATER NATIONAL WILDLIFE REFUGE, CAMBRIDGE, MARYLAND • ABOVE: UPPER THOROFARE, DEAL ISLAND, MARYLAND

Tidal Marshes

At the meeting of land and water, two ecosystems collaborate to create a natural work of art. The Blackwater National Wildlife Refuge is a spectacular vantage point to observe thousands of migratory waterfowl. The 27,000-acre area is composed mainly of tidal salt marshes and offers hiking and paddling trails, cycling roads, and hunting and fishing.

Deal Island Bridge

Tiny Deal Island remains untouched by the sprawl of modernism. Just beyond the Deal Island Bridge, visitors will observe an oyster hatchery, crab pickers at the harbor, and fishermen unloading the day's catch. Deal Island Harbor is home to the Annual Skipjack Races. Migrating waterfowl are a big attraction at the Deal Island Wildlife Management Area.

TOP AND BOTTOM: SOMERS COVE, LITTLE ANNEMESSEX RIVER, CRISFIELD, MARYLAND

Crisfield

New waterfront condominiums have risen in Crisfield, the southernmost city in Maryland, near the mouth of the Little Annemessex River. Nearly half of the city's topography is water, and most of Crisfield was built on billions of oyster shells, crushed together to fill the swampland. Since the introduction of the railroad in the mid-1800s, Crisfield has supplied seafood to many important markets of the Northeast. Today, the harbor of Somers Cove is home to the largest state-owned marina in Maryland. Ferries to Smith and Tangier islands and hundreds of work boats travel in and out of the harbor carrying passengers, oysters, crabs, and other seafood.

SMITH ISLAND, MARYLAND

Soft Shell Crab Capital

Sighted by Captain John Smith and settled by English watermen in the 1600s, Smith Island still is accessible only by boat. Some inhabitants retain the Elizabethan dialect of their ancestors. Smith Island earned the title of "soft shell crab capital of the world." A visit to Ewell, the island's largest community, is the quintessential Chesapeake Bay experience.

TOP: SMITH ISLAND, MARYLAND • BOTTOM: TANGIER ISLAND, VIRGINIA

Isolated Tangier Island

Tangier Island, 6 miles below the Maryland-Virginia State line, remains isolated from the mainland even in the modern day. The only access to the island is via boat or small aircraft. Crabbing, oystering, and tourism are the island's main livelihoods. Visitors can catch a cruise across beautiful Tangier Sound and explore the island's famous water trails.

OPPOSITE: COD HARBOR, TANGIER ISLAND, VIRGINIA • TOP: CAPE CHARLES, VIRGINIA • BOTTOM: KIPTOPEKE STATE PARK, CAPE CHARLES, VIRGINIA

Isolated Ecosystem

In 1608, Captain John Smith came upon a group of marshy islands, which he named the Russell Isles. Today, the group is known separately as Smith, Tangier, and Watts islands. Tangier remains relatively isolated from the mainland. It is known for the unusual dialect of its residents as well as its wonderful seafood dishes, especially the soft-shell crab sandwiches.

Victoriana

Cape Charles was founded in 1884 by ferry and railroad interests and was an important passenger and car ferry terminal until the construction of the Chesapeake Bay Bridge-Tunnel. Cape Charles has one of the largest concentrations of late-Victorian and turn-of-the-century buildings on the East Coast and is on the National Register of Historic Places.

Kiptopeke Cabins

Kiptopeke State Park provides recreational access to the Chesapeake Bay. Besides cabins, yurts, and RV campsites, it has a public beach, a fishing pier, trails, educational programs, and a rich bird habitat along the Atlantic Flyway. Kiptopeke, meaning "Big Water," was named by Captain John Smith to honor a royal member of the Accawmacke Indian tribe.

OPPOSITE: CAPE CHARLES LIGHTHOUSE, SMITH ISLAND, VIRGINIA • ABOVE: CHESAPEAKE BAY BRIDGE-TUNNEL, VIRGINA

Cape Charles Light

Standing just over 192 feet, the Cape Charles Lighthouse is the second tallest in the United States. Completed in 1895 and operated manually until its automation in 1963, it marks the northern entrance to the Chesapeake Bay. Cape Charles Light is owned and maintained by the United States Coast Guard and continues to aide the region's coastal navigation.

Chesapeake Bay Bridge-Tunnel

A modern engineering wonder, the Chesapeake Bay Bridge-Tunnel provides a direct link between southeastern Virginia and the Delmarva Peninsula. Crossing over and under the open waters where the Chesapeake Bay and the Atlantic Ocean meet, this 20-mile-long structure represents both form and function on one of the world's most beautiful waterways.

Jake McGuire is known for his striking photographs of American cities and landscapes. His works often appear in private and corporate collections, exhibitions, and airline and travel magazines. He has won 11 awards for photography and photojournalism. In 1989, the Presidential Inaugural Committee commissioned McGuire to produce a limited edition print of the White House, to be signed by the President and Vice President and presented to the Inaugural Gala performers. In 1992, McGuire received an Arts America grant from the United States Information Agency to give photography lectures in the Persian Gulf Sheikdom of Bahrain. In 1997, *LIFE MAGAZINE* selected one of McGuire's photos for a special edition cover. In 2004, the Presidential Inaugural Committee chose McGuire's images for official inaugural publications. The same year, Jake McGuire joined forces with Twin Lights Publishers to produce a series of colorful photographic albums. Titles that are currently available, include *Washington, D.C.: A Photographic Portrait, Baltimore, MD: A Photographic Portrait, Annapolis, MD: A Photographic Portrait, Tidewater, VA: A Photographic Portrait,* and *Flying Above the New England Coast.* See more about Jake's work at www.themcguirecollection.com.

Anna Katalkina, born in St. Petersburg, Russia, is an accomplished artist and linguist who works with private and corporate collections in the United States and abroad. She manages photo shoots, edits photographs, researches and writes the text for many of Jake McGuire's beautiful books, and her own fine art photography of Europe is part of the McGuire Collection.